The Jane Austen

MISCELLANY

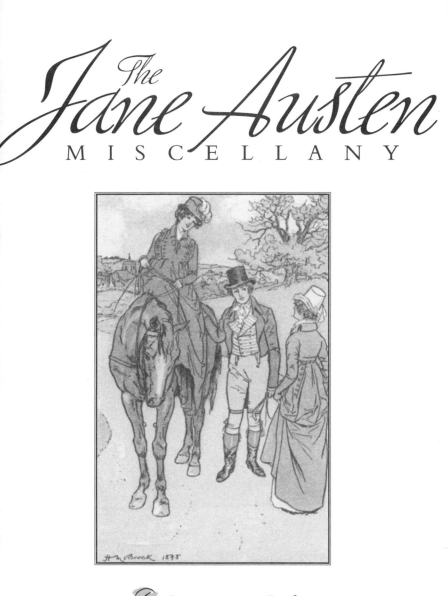

SOURCEBOOKS, INC.®
NAPERVILLE, ILLINOIS

Copyright © 2006 by Sourcebooks, Inc.
Cover and internal design © 2006 by Sourcebooks, Inc.
Cover illustration by Charles Edmund Brock
Sourcebooks and the colophon are registered trademarks of Sourcebooks, Inc
Compiled by Lesley Bolton

Published by Sourcebooks, Inc.
P.O. Box 4410, Naperville, Illinois 60567-4410
(630) 961-3900
Fax: (630) 961-2168
www.sourcebooks.com

Library of Congress Cataloging-in-Publication Data

The Jane Austen Miscellany / compiled by Lesley Bolton.
    p. cm.
 ISBN-13: 978-1-4022-0685-6
 ISBN-10: 1-4022-0685-2
 1. Austen, Jane, 1775-1817—Miscellanea. I. Bolton, Lesley.

PR4032.I23 2006
823'.7—dc22

2005033339

Printed and bound in the United States of America
LB 10 9 8 7 6 5 4 3 2 1

Introduction

Jane Austen's entire body of published work is comprised of a mere six novels. Faithful readers have read them all. In fact, they've read them all more than once. In fact, they reread them on an annual basis.

For those who seek more, here in this book you will find quotes from your favorite characters, the barbed wit of Jane herself, trivia and tidbits from Jane's life and times, and a peek at the world of film and print that pays homage to Jane.

A note about the illustrators: Charles Edmund Brock and his brother, Henry Matthew Brock, provided illustrations for many of the most popular books published on the cusp of the twentieth century. C.E. Brock completed illustrations for *Pride and Prejudice* in 1895, *Sense and Sensibility* in 1906, and various illustrations for *Emma, Northanger Abbey, Mansfield Park,* and *Persuasion* in 1907 and 1908. Both Charles and Henry provided illustrations for the six novels in the 1906 anthology *The Novels and Letters of Jane Austen* (Manor House Edition, edited by R. Brimley Johnson). The two brothers shared a studio and were sources of great inspiration to one another.

ON DECEMBER 16, 1775, *Jane Austen, one of the world's greatest novelists, was born. She was the seventh child born to Reverend George Austen and his wife, Cassandra. Having produced only six novels, she is nonetheless regarded as one of the most popular authors ever to come from England. Her novels, letters, and minor works have both touched the hearts of casual readers and exercised the brains of scholars. She is at the same time accessible and untouchable, and she has inspired a veritable industry of sequels, adaptations, movies, and miniseries.*

"We have all a better guide in ourselves, if we would attend to it, than any other person can be."

—*Fanny Price in* Mansfield Park

"She was very attractive; her figure was rather tall and slender, her step light and firm, and her whole appearance expressive of health and animation. In complexion she was a clear brunette with a rich colour; she had full round cheeks, with mouth and nose small and well formed, bright hazel eyes, and brown hair forming natural curls close round her face."

—*James Edward Austen-Leigh, describing his aunt Jane*

THE *Juvenilia*

Love and Freindship [sic] (written between 1790 and 1792) is a parody of society's enthusiasm for sensibility in which characters suffer great emotional outbursts and fatal fainting fits. The story opens with a letter from Isabel to Laura: "How often, in answer to my repeated entreaties that you would give my Daughter a regular detail of the Misfortunes and Adventures of your Life, have you said 'No, my freind [sic], never will I comply with your request till I may be no longer in Danger of again experiencing such dreadful ones.'"

Jane's WORLD

During the Regency period, use of laudanum was quite rampant. Jane Austen showed the ill effects of drug abuse by the upper classes in the form of the perpetually doped, comically loopy Lady Bertram in *Mansfield Park*. The Prince Regent was also known to be fond of laudanum, imbibing about 250 drops a day!

FURTHER READING FOR THOSE WHO CAN'T GET ENOUGH

Mr. Darcy Takes a Wife and *Darcy & Elizabeth*
by Linda Berdoll (2004 and 2006)
These sequels to *Pride and Prejudice* offer an intimate look at life at Pemberley in an epic, romantic, and often funny way. With lots of sex and some violence, they may be a bit risqué for Austen purists, but the realistic, human view of the Darcys makes each a great read.

Jane's Life

"There was one gentleman, an officer of the Cheshire, a very good-looking young man, who, I was told, wanted very much to be introduced to me, but as he did not want it quite enough to take much trouble in effecting it, we never could bring it about."

—from a letter to her sister dated January 8, 1799

IN 1773, *Cassandra Elizabeth Austen, Jane's only sister, was born. Cassandra and Jane were so close that they wrote to one another every day whenever they were apart. Austen fans have Cassandra to thank not only for most of Jane's surviving letters, but also for the only verified portrait of Jane. Cassandra wrote to her niece following Jane's death: "I have lost a treasure, such a sister, such a friend as never can have been surpassed. She was the sun of my life, the gilder of every pleasure, the soother of every sorrow; I had not a thought concealed from her, and it is as if I had lost a part of myself."*

MARRIAGE AND MATTERS OF *the Heart*

"Where people wish to attach, they should always be igno-rant. To come with a well-informed mind is to come with an inability of administering to the vanity of others, which a sensible person would always wish to avoid. A woman especially, if she have the misfortune of knowing any thing, should conceal it as well as she can."

—*from* Northanger Abbey

UP CLOSE AND *Personal*

A Memoir of Jane Austen

by James Austen-Leigh (1870)

An inside look into the private life of our beloved author, including details even of the tone of her voice. This mem-oir gathers the recollections of Jane's nephew James, his two sisters, and Jane's brother Henry, and is considered to be the authority on Jane's life.

Mr Denny introduces his friend.
Chap XV

Pride and Prejudice

THE FABRIC OF LIFE:
Fashion and Manners

"I cannot help thinking that it is more natural to have flowers grow out of the head than fruit. What do you think on that subject?"

—*from a letter to her sister concerning purchasing a sprig for a hat*

FURTHER READING FOR THOSE WHO CAN'T GET ENOUGH

The Diary of Henry Fitzwilliam Darcy
by Marjorie Fasman (1997)
As a companion to *Pride and Prejudice*, the story is told through the eyes of Mr. Darcy in the form of a diary. Detailing his most personal thoughts and feelings, the first diary entry begins at the age of ten and continues beyond Darcy and Elizabeth's wedding.

JANE'S FAVORITE *Heroine*

Austen said of Elizabeth Bennet of *Pride and Prejudice*: "I think her as delightful a creature as ever appeared in print, and how I shall be able to tolerate those who do not like her at least I do not know."

OUR *Hero*

Mr. Darcy in *Pride and Prejudice* has his faults—pride, arrogance, aloofness, and a touch of snobbery—but this only heightens his appeal. Tall, dark, and handsome, though certainly fitting, does not do justice to this heart-fluttering characterization of a true man.

THE FABRIC OF LIFE: *Fashion and Manners*

"I learnt from Mrs. Tickars's young lady, to my high amusement, that the stays [corsets] now are not made to force the bosom up at all; that was a very unbecoming, unnatural fashion. I was really glad to hear that they are not to be so much off the shoulders as they were."

—from a letter to her sister

Jane's Life

Jane was not immune to youthful flirtations but did not take them seriously. In a letter to her sister dated January 16, 1796, she writes rather sarcastically, "The day is come on which I am to flirt my last with Tom Lefroy, and when you receive this it will be over. My tears flow as I write at the melancholy idea."

FURTHER READING FOR THOSE WHO CAN'T GET ENOUGH

Perfect Happiness

by Rachel Billington (1996)

Taking its title from the last line of *Emma*, this novel continues Emma's story one year after her marriage to Mr. Knightley, questioning the happy-ever-after ending.

AUSTENIAN *Insults*

"The person, be it gentleman or lady, who has not pleasure in a good novel, must be intolerably stupid."

—*Henry Tilney in* Northanger Abbey

"She very soon heard Captain Wentworth and Louisa"
Chapter X.

Persuasion

MARRIAGE AND MATTERS OF *the Heart*

"[Miss Bigg] writes me word that Miss Blackford is married, but I have never seen it in the papers, and one may as well be single if the wedding is not to be in print."

—from a letter to her sister

FURTHER READING FOR THOSE WHO CAN'T GET ENOUGH

Desire and Duty
by Ted and Marilyn Bader (1997)
In this sequel to *Pride and Prejudice*, shy Georgiana Darcy's narrow escape from the clutches of Mr. Wickham causes her to be apprehensive as she yearns to love and be loved.

Virginia Woolf called Jane Austen
"the most perfect artist among women."

AT THE *Movies*

Northanger Abbey (1986)

A melodramatic adaptation in which the impressionable Catherine Morland (played by Katharine Schlesinger) experiences many gothic fantasies as her imagination side-steps reality. The eerie daydreams are juxtaposed with the beauty of opulent costumes, lush settings, and the charming Henry Tilney (played by Peter Firth).

"What should I do with your strong, manly, spirited Sketches, full of Variety and Glow?—How could I join them on to the little bit (two Inches wide) of Ivory on which I work with so fine a Brush, as produces little effect after much labour?"

—*from a letter to her nephew James Edward Austen-Leigh*

THE FABRIC OF LIFE:
Fashion and Manners

"A girl not out has always the same sort of dress: a close bonnet, for instance; looks very demure, and never says a word. You may smile, but it is so, I assure you; and except that it is sometimes carried a little too far, it is all very proper. Girls should be quiet and modest. The most objectionable part is that the alteration of manners on being introduced into company is frequently too sudden."

—*Miss Crawford in* Mansfield Park

Trivia

Northanger Abbey was sold to a publisher named Crosby in 1803. Crosby advertised it as forthcoming, but he kept it on his shelves for many years, never actually publishing it. He sold the copy back to Jane's brother Henry for the same amount he bought it, and Henry finally published it after Jane's death.

"How do you like my gown?"
Chapter XXXVIII

Emma

FURTHER READING FOR THOSE WHO CAN'T GET ENOUGH

Lady Catherine's Necklace
by Joan Aiken (2000)
This continuation of *Pride and Prejudice* turns the spotlight to the socially powerful snob Lady Catherine de Bourgh. A carriage accident brings the Delaval siblings to Rosings, unleashing a scandalous chain of events and revelations, including the kidnapping of Lady Catherine.

THE FABRIC OF LIFE:
Fashion and Manners

"A bride, you know, must appear like a bride, but my natural taste is all for simplicity; a simple style of dress is so infinitely preferable to finery. But I am quite in the minority, I believe; few people seem to value simplicity of dress—show and finery are everything."

—*Mrs. Elton in* Emma

 WORLD

Home remedies were popular during Jane's time. When Jane contracted whooping cough, the advice of her sister-in-law, Martha Lloyd, was to "cut off the hair from the top of the head as large as a crown piece. Take a piece of brown paper of the same size: dip it in rectified oyl of amber, and apply it to the part for nine mornings, dipping the paper fresh every morning."

Trivia

In every one of Jane's longer novels (save for *Northanger Abbey*), a major turning point, climax, or event occurs on a Tuesday.

THE *Juvenilia*

The History of England (written between 1790 and 1792) by "a partial, prejudiced, and ignorant Historian" is a rewrite (Austen-style) of classroom history books, improved by the inclusion of more women and her own take on England's great leaders. The text begins with Henry IV: "Henry the 4th ascended the throne of England much to his own satisfaction in the year 1399, after having prevailed on his cousin & predecessor Richard the 2nd to resign it to him, & to retire for the rest of his Life to Pomfret Castle, where he happened to be murdered."

Jane's Life

As the writer of some of the greatest romances ever, Austen had very little personal experience from which to draw. Aside from a few flirtations, her only brush with romantic love happened along a seashore with an unnamed man. According to her sister Cassandra, the young man was a worthy suitor and likely would have been successful with Jane. When they parted, he made his intentions to meet with the sisters in the future quite clear. However, news of his death reached them shortly after. No account of Jane's reaction upon receiving the news has been noted, though some believe this experience finds its way into PERSUASION.

UP CLOSE AND *Personal*

The Making of Pride and Prejudice

by Sue Birtwistle and Susie Conklin (1995)

A companion book to the BBC/A&E production of *Pride and Prejudice,* featuring such gems as casting stories, behind-the-scenes pictures (many of Colin Firth), and setting creations.

Jane's Life

Jane's eldest brother, James, was "good and clever," according to Jane. He was fond of writing poetry that referenced nature, but he failed in his literary ambitions, while watching his sister succeed in hers.

AT THE *Movies*

Mansfield Park (1986)

This BBC miniseries production lacks the dramatic glamour of its Hollywood counterpart, but true Austen fans will appreciate the fact that this adaptation remains faithful to the novel, recognizing that Austen doesn't need to be dressed up to be beautiful.

FURTHER READING FOR THOSE WHO CAN'T GET ENOUGH

Emma in Love

by Emma Tennant (1996)

A controversial sequel to *Emma* that emanates overtones of homosexuality. Bored in her fourth year of marriage, Emma seeks out leisure pursuits to amuse herself.

"Henry drove so well"
Chap XX

Northanger Abbey

THE FABRIC OF LIFE:
Fashion and Manners

A "palisse" is a cross between a coat and a dress, and was typically worn over a long cotton dress. Hampshire Museum Services currently has a palisse that is said to have been worn by Jane and was donated by her older brother James's great-great-great-grandchild. Reflective of the fashions during her time, the dress coat features an oak leaf pattern, a high standing collar, close-fitting sleeves, ruching and cording trim, and silk lining.

Jane's Life

Though Jane openly admitted her hatred of the Prince Regent in a letter dated February 16, 1813, she did her duty and dedicated EMMA to him at his request.

AUSTENIAN *Insults*

"Be careful not to expect too much beauty."

—from a letter to her sister

THE *Juvenilia*

Lesley Castle (written between 1790 and 1792) is a humorous story with several subplots containing such scandals as divorce, remarriage, and an adulterous affair. The story begins with Miss Margaret Lesley's letter to Miss Charlotte Lutterell: "Brother has just left us. 'Matilda' (said he at parting) 'you and Margaret will I am certain take all the care of my dear little one, that she might have received from an indulgent, an affectionate, an amiable Mother.' Tears rolled down his cheeks as he spoke these words—the remembrance of her, who had so wantonly disgraced the Maternal character and so openly violated the conjugal Duties, prevented his adding anything farther."

THE FABRIC OF LIFE:
Fashion and Manners

"She is perfectly well-bred, indeed, and has the air of a woman of fashion, but her Manners are not such as can persuade me of her being prepossessed in my favour."

—*Lady Susan Vernon in* Lady Susan

"There is nothing like employment, active indispensible employment, for relieving sorrow."

—*from* Mansfield Park

Jane's Life

While many scholars have commented on Austen's sheltered life, she was not immune to tragedy within the family. In 1794, the Comte de Feuillide, the husband of her cousin Eliza, was guillotined in Paris shortly after the French Revolution, causing Eliza to take up residence with the Austens.

In *Northanger Abbey*, Catherine Morland allows her imagination to run roughshod over her common sense and propriety. The fuel for her fantasy came from Ann Radcliffe's *The Mysteries of Udolpho*, a gothic novel of terror and suspense. Although the book was quite popular at the time, Jane Austen herself was known to dislike Radcliffe's work.

MARRIAGE AND MATTERS OF *the Heart*

"To be so bent on marriage—to pursue a man merely for the sake of situation—is a sort of thing that shocks me; I cannot understand it. Poverty is a great evil, but to a woman of education and feeling it ought not, it cannot be the greatest—I would rather be a teacher at a school (and I can think of nothing worse) than marry a man I did not like."

—*Emma in* The Watsons

FURTHER READING FOR THOSE WHO CAN'T GET ENOUGH

The Third Sister

by Julia Barrett (1996)

In this sequel to *Sense and Sensibility*, the elder sisters have married and moved away, but their traumatic experiences in courtship stay with Margaret as she stumbles along trying to find her own way in life and love.

"I fancy I am rather a favourite; he took notice of my gown."

—*Mrs. Elton in* Emma

"She describes men and women exactly as men and women really are."

—*Lord Brabourne on Jane Austen*

" Drove her into a fainting fit "

Chapter XXXVII

Sense and Sensibility

Jane's Life

Jane earned only about 630 pounds from her works during her lifetime, but the money was important to her: "I have now written myself into two hundred and fifty pounds which only makes me long for more."

—from a letter to her brother Frank

Jane's WORLD

Novels came to be regarded as trash, as wicked influences on the minds of young women. Austen takes up the fight in *Northanger Abbey* and defends the novel by saying it is the work "in which the greatest powers of the mind are displayed, in which the most thorough knowledge of human nature, the happiest delineation of its varieties, the liveliest effusions of wit and humour, are conveyed to the world in the best-chosen language."

"Read again, for the third time at least, Miss Austen's finely written novel of *Pride and Prejudice*. That young Lady had a talent for describing the involvements and feelings and characters of ordinary life, which is to me the most wonderful I ever met with. The big Bow-Wow strain I can do myself like any now going; but the exquisite touch which renders ordinary common-place things and characters interesting from the truth of the description and the sentiment is denied to me. What a pity such a gifted creature died so early!"

—*from Sir Walter Scott's diary*

"There is no story in it, except that Miss Emma found that the man whom she designed for Harriet's lover was an admirer of her own—& he was affronted at being refused by Emma."

—*Maria Edgeworth, an Irish novelist whom Austen greatly admired, on* Emma

UP CLOSE AND *Personal*

Jane Austen's Letters
by Deirdre Le Faye (third edition, 1997)
Offering an inside glimpse that only Austen can provide, the letters from Austen to her family (particularly her sister) and friends detail her daily life and events, complete with gossip and witty observations—all told through that unmistakable voice that we cherish.

AUSTENIAN *Insults*

"She appeared exactly as she did in September, with the same broad face, diamond bandeau, white shoes, pink husband, and fat neck."

—*from a letter to her sister*

AT THE *Movies*

Pride and Prejudice (1940)

Though the costumes are way off (more reflective of the U.S. Civil War era), they seem to work in this adaptation—or maybe it's just that we've been awestruck by the dashing Laurence Olivier as Mr. Darcy and the beautiful and charming Greer Garson as Elizabeth Bennet.

"Pictures of perfection make me sick and wicked."

—from a letter to Fanny Knight

Jane's WORLD

Dancing was very popular during Jane's time as it offered the perfect (and in some cases, the only) opportunity for flirtations and courtship. Jane loved to dance and referred to it often in letters to her sister: "There were twenty dances, and I danced them all, and without any fatigue."

"You must allow me to present this young lady to you"
Chap. VI

Pride and Prejudice

Jane's WORLD

The West Indies and the slaves there were a very profitable resource for Britain. Several of Jane's relatives relied on the West Indies for their income. This reliance was reflected in the character of Sir Thomas Bertram in *Mansfield Park*.

FURTHER READING FOR THOSE WHO CAN'T GET ENOUGH

Pride and Promiscuity
by Arielle Eckstut and Dennis Ashton (2001)
A collection of "lost sex scenes" from Austen's novels. Austen's most notable characters—including, unfortunately, the far-from-sexy Mr. Collins—are placed in compromising and saucy situations. Not recommended for the fainthearted.

Trivia

Jane Austen was listed in *People* magazine's Most Intriguing People list in 1995.

"For what do we live, but to make sport for our neighbours, and laugh at them in our turn?"

—*Mr. Bennet in* Pride and Prejudice

Jane's WORLD

Since all well-bred young ladies were expected to be musically inclined, particularly on the pianoforte, music was always present at gatherings during which young ladies could display their talents for potential suitors. If you wonder what sort of music they played, there are several compilations of music that would have been played during that time period, such as *Piano Classics from the World of Jane Austen* (Karlyn Bond, 1996).

Trivia

In the 1986 television version of *Northanger Abbey*, the characters bathe in Roman baths, which were not discovered in England until seventy years after the story's setting.

"I could no more write a [historical] romance than an epic poem. I could not sit seriously down to write a serious romance under any other motive than to save my life; and if it were indispensable for me to keep it up and never relax into laughing at myself or at other people, I am sure I should be hung before I had finished the first chapter."

—Austen's response to the proposal of a new project

FURTHER READING FOR THOSE WHO CAN'T GET ENOUGH

Pride and Prescience
by Carrie Bebris (2004)
Pride and Prejudice continues with this whodunit story complete with murder, madness, and possibly magic.

THE *Juvenilia*

Henry and Eliza (written between 1787 and 1790) is a tale with an extraordinary heroine who takes on the role of a hero, complete with armed battle. The story opens with "As Sir George & Lady Harcourt were superintending the Labours of their Haymakers, rewarding the industry of some by smiles of approbation, & punishing the idleness of others, by a cudgel, they perceived lying closely concealed beneath the thick foliage of a Haycock, a beautiful little Girl not more than three months old."

THE FABRIC OF LIFE: *Fashion and Manners*

In the first surviving letter to her sister Cassandra, Jane spills the beans about her flirtation with an Irishman: "I am almost afraid to tell you how my Irish friend and I behaved. Imagine to yourself everything most profligate and shocking in the way of dancing and sitting down together. I can expose myself however, only *once more,* because he leaves the country soon after next Friday, on which day we are to have a dance at Ashe after all."

"*I planned the match from that hour*"
Chapter I

Emma

"There will be little rubs and disappointments everywhere, and we are all apt to expect too much; but then, if one scheme of happiness fails, human nature turns to another; if the first calculation is wrong, we make a second better: we find comfort somewhere."

—*Mrs. Grant in* Mansfield Park

FURTHER READING FOR THOSE WHO CAN'T GET ENOUGH

Letters from Pemberley the First Year
by Jane Dawkins (2003)
Pride and Prejudice continues with a compilation of letters from the newly married Elizabeth Darcy to her beloved (and also newly married!) sister Jane Bingley, detailing the trials and joys of her new life of wealth and privilege.

THE FABRIC OF LIFE:
Fashion and Manners

A man never sat next to a lady in a carriage unless he was her husband or a relative. He always sat in the seat facing backward and descended first to help the lady out.

Jane composed several prayers, but only three remain. An abridged version of one hangs on the wall of St. Nicholas Church in Steventon, which was her father's parish. In it she writes: "Have we thought irreverently of thee, have we disobeyed thy commandments, have we neglected any known duty, or willingly given pain to any human being? Incline us to ask our hearts these questions oh! God, to save us from deceiving ourselves by pride or vanity."

"Handsome is as Handsome does; he is therefore a very ill-looking man."

—*from a letter to her sister*

Jane's Life

None of the novels published during Jane's lifetime gave her credit as author. Instead, the title page of SENSE AND SENSIBILITY *stated it was* "By a Lady." *Her next,* PRIDE AND PREJUDICE, *gave credit to* "The Author of SENSE AND SENSIBILITY." *The others followed in the same manner.*

"Anything like warmth or enthusiasm; anything energetic, poignant, heartfelt, is utterly out of place in commending [Austen's] works."

—*Charlotte Brontë*

FURTHER READING FOR THOSE WHO CAN'T GET ENOUGH

Bridget Jones' Diary and *Bridget Jones: The Edge of Reason* by Helen Fielding (1998 and 2000)

In these modern spin-offs of *Pride and Prejudice*, Bridget Jones confronts life as a "singleton," wading through lust and love—one of her objects of lust being Colin Firth as Fitzwilliam Darcy: "We all fell silent then, watching Colin Firth emerging from the lake dripping wet, in the see-through white shirt. Mmm. Mmmm." In the movie adaptations of *Bridget Jones*, Colin Firth plays a parallel role as Mark Darcy.

"He could not help giving Mrs Norris a hint"
Chap. XX.

Mansfield Park

"...the want of moral illumination on the part of [Jane Austen's] heroines, who had undoubtedly small and second-rate minds and were perfect little she-Philistines. But I think that is partly what makes them interesting today."

—*Henry James*

"[Austen's novels] appear to be compact of abject truth. Their events are excruciatingly unimportant; and yet, with *R. Crusoe*, they will probably outlast all Fielding, Scott, George Eliot, Thackeray, and Dickens. The art is so consummate that the secret is hidden; peer at them as hard as one may; shake them; take them apart; one cannot see how it is done."

—*Thornton Wilder*

"She is one of the most consistent satirists in the whole of literature."

—*Virginia Woolf*

Jane's Life

Religion was a pervasive aspect of Jane Austen's life. She is known to have written evening prayers for her father's services. One such prayer begins: "Almighty God! Look down with mercy on thy servants here assembled and accept the petitions now offered up unto thee. Pardon oh! God the offences of the past day. We are conscious of many frailties; we remember with shame and contrition, many evil thoughts and neglected duties; and we have perhaps sinned against thee and against our fellow-creatures in many instances of which we have no remembrance."

UP CLOSE AND *Personal*

The Life of Jane Austen

by John Halperin (with new preface, 1996)

This controversial biography debunks the idea of an all-smiles, continuously cheerful Jane. The author tosses Austen from her pedestal, placing her on an even playing field with all other human beings in pointing out her problems with family, friends, suitors, and her career.

AT THE *Movies*

Sense and Sensibility (1995)

Emma Thompson not only starred in the film as the sensible Elinor but also wrote the smart and witty screenplay. This adaptation takes liberties with the story line to fill in some gaps but makes up for everything by starring Hugh Grant as the shy Edmund Ferrars, Kate Winslet as the wild Marianne, and Alan Rickman as the steadfast Colonel Brandon.

"I give you joy of our new nephew, and hope if he ever comes to be hanged it will not be till we are too old to care about it."

—from a letter to her sister

"Miss Austen was surely a great novelist. What she did, she did perfectly. Her work, as far as it goes, is faultless. It is not that her people are all good—and, certainly, they are not all wise. The faults of some are the anvils on which the virtues of others are hammered till they are bright as steel."

—Anthony Trollope

UP CLOSE AND *Personal*

Jane Austen: A Life
by David Nokes (1997)

Offering an alternate perspective, this biography focuses on Austen as the "wild beast" she claimed to be. Austen's family is portrayed as manipulative and their misdeeds brought to light.

Jane's Life

Jane's brother Frank joined the navy at age twelve and fought in the Napoleonic Wars, just missing the Battle of Trafalgar. He was later knighted as Sir Francis Austen.

IN 1764, *Reverend George Austen married Cassandra Leigh. Because each came from the poorer branches of their families, they were only able to marry with the generosity and donations of Austen's wealthier relatives. His distant cousin Thomas Knight gave Austen the Steventon rectory and a stipend, and his uncle Francis Austen gave him the Deane rectory that Austen eventually rented out.*

THE FABRIC OF LIFE:
Fashion and Manners

When a gentleman met a lady in the street, he was not supposed to speak to her until she had spoken to him first.

Trivia

The title of *Persuasion* was not chosen by Jane Austen, as it was published posthumously. There was some speculation she intended to call this novel *The Elliots*.

Jane's WORLD

Bathing in the Regency period, when Jane Austen lived and wrote, was a scarce practice. When the nobility did bathe, it was most likely in portable tubs, in which they were doused with buckets of warmed water by their servants. Women as well as men bathed infrequently and both used makeup, perfume, and dark clothing to cover their lack of cleanliness.

A *Rousing* MOMENT

Though Austen was careful to avoid interjecting steamy scenes of passion into her novels, she did allow herself (and the reader) a few rousing moments: "Emma understood him; and as soon as she could recover from the flutter of pleasure excited by such tender consideration, replied, 'You are very kind—but you are mistaken, and I must set you right—I am not in want of that sort of compassion.'"

—*from* Emma

THE *Juvenilia*

The Beautifull Cassandra (written between 1787 and 1790) is a parody of the melodramatic novels of the time and tells the story of a young woman who braves the world to find her fortune. Chapter the First in its entirety is: "Cassandra was the Daughter and the only Daughter of a celebrated Milliner in Bond Street. Her father was of noble Birth, being the near relation of the Dutchess of —'s Butler."

"The kitchen-garden was to be next admired"
Chap XXII

Northanger Abbey

AUSTENIAN *Insults*

"The pleasures of Vanity are more within your comprehension."

—from a letter to Fanny Knight

Jane's WORLD

Gretna Green, a Scottish village on the England-Scotland border, was the hot spot for elopements for all sorts of people. However, popularity waned when a bill was passed in 1856 that voided marriages in Gretna Green unless one of the parties was a resident of Scotland for at least twenty-one days prior to the marriage. In *Pride and Prejudice*, Lydia leaves a note saying she is going to Gretna Green with "an angel," which is really her bounder boyfriend Wickham.

"[Jane Austen's] greatness is due precisely to the fact that her attitude toward her work is like that of a man, that is, of an artist, and quite unlike that of the typical woman novelist, who exploits her feminine day dreams…She is, in my opinion, one of the half dozen greatest English writers."

—*Edmund Wilson*

Trivia

Jane Austen wrote her last will and testament in 1817 at her Chawton home in Hampshire. Her assets totaled somewhere under 800 pounds ($1,540.50 in U.S. dollars), and she left just about everything to her only sister, Cassandra. But because the will was not signed by witnesses, two of Jane's friends had to write a statement swearing they had known her for years and recognized her handwriting.

The devotion of Jane Austen's fans can be seen in the number of Jane Austen Societies in existence, including the Jane Austen Society of North America, which publishes a periodical called *Persuasions.*

THE FABRIC OF LIFE:
Fashion and Manners

Austen's comical portrayal of appropriate social behavior goes beyond poking fun at proper manners by following the stimulating waltz of courtship: "To be fond of dancing was a certain step towards falling in love; and very lively hopes of Mr. Bingley's heart were entertained."

—*from* Pride and Prejudice

Trivia

In the 1971 television miniseries version of *Persuasion,* the characters, walking down a country lane, pass World War II tank traps.

MARRIAGE AND MATTERS OF *the Heart*

Jane Austen's mother, Cassandra (Leigh) Austen, came from a distinguished and ancient family that was linked to Thomas Leigh, a lord mayor of London during the reign of Elizabeth I. It is thought that Jane inherited some of her wit, humor, and writing skill from her mother. Cassandra's granddaughter noted that she was "a quick-witted woman with plenty of sparkle and spirit in her talk who could write an excellent letter in either prose or verse with no pretence to poetry but simply common sense in rhyme."

THE FABRIC OF LIFE: *Fashion and Manners*

Men's fashions in the Regency period, as with women's fashions, were simpler and less ornate than preceding periods. Men wore darker colors and breeches and boots rather than stockings and buckled shoes. They also forsook the powdered wig in favor of their own natural short hair.

" Of all the consequence in their power "

Chapter XX

Persuasion

UP CLOSE AND *Personal*

Jane Austen: A Life
by Claire Tomalin (1999)
A biography of Austen that connects her writings to the social circumstances of the time and follows her growth as a writer. The author expands on the biographical information by including details of extended family members and even neighbors.

AUSTENIAN *Insults*

"He was not handsome, and his manners required intimacy to make them pleasing."

—*from* Sense and Sensibility

Trivia

The Austen family coat of arms was inscribed with the following Latin quote: *Qui invidit minor est*, which translates "Whoever envies me is lesser than I."

Winston Churchill, when ordered to refrain from work and to rest, had Jane Austen's *Pride and Prejudice* read to him. He said, "I had long ago read Jane Austen's *Sense and Sensibility*, and now I thought I would have *Pride and Prejudice*…What calm lives they had, those people! No worries about the French Revolution, or the crashing struggle of the Napoleonic Wars. Only manners controlling natural passion as far as they could, together with cultured explanations of any mischances."

FURTHER READING FOR THOSE WHO CAN'T GET ENOUGH

Jane Austen's Guide to Dating
by Lauren Hendersen (2005)
This book takes two-hundred-year-old wit, wisdom, and perception on matters of the heart and applies it to the modern-day dating scene. Summarizing love stories from many of Austen's novels, Hendersen's explanations of lessons learned are valuable to singles everywhere. A list of dos and don'ts and a collection of quizzes help you find out which Austen character you are.

AUSTENIAN *Insults*

"There certainly were a dreadful multitude of ugly women in Bath; and as for the men! they were infinitely worse."

—*from* Persuasion

JANE AUSTEN LITERARY *Walk*

A "Jane Austen Literary Walk from Chawton to Farringdon" is available in Hampshire, England. This walk is thought to be reminiscent of the many walks that Elizabeth Bennet takes to Meryton in *Pride and Prejudice*. Further information can be obtained by visiting www.easthants.gov.uk.

MARRIAGE AND MATTERS OF *the Heart*

"A last and indubitable proof of Warren's indifference to me…he actually drew that gentleman's picture for me, and delivered it to me without a sigh."

—*from a letter to her sister*

"I am at a loss to understand why people hold Miss Austen's novels at so high a rate, which seem to me vulgar in tone, sterile in artistic invention, imprisoned in their wretched conventions of English society, without genius, wit, or knowledge of the world. Never was life so pinched and narrow…All that interests in any character [is this]: has he (or she) the money to marry with?…Suicide is more respectable."

—*Ralph Waldo Emerson*

FURTHER READING FOR THOSE WHO CAN'T GET ENOUGH

Vanity and Vexation
by Kate Fenton (2004)
In this modern retelling of *Pride and Prejudice*, the gender roles are reversed against the backdrop of the filming of *Pride and Prejudice*. As the plot unfolds, it becomes an exploration of what happens when two powerful, wealthy women (film director and movie star) meet two modest local chaps (writer and carpenter) and fall in love.

THE FABRIC OF LIFE:
Fashion and Manners

The high-waisted gowns worn by Jane Austen and her female characters are known as empire style. It was said to have been inspired by Josephine Bonaparte and was based on the classical Grecian robe style.

"I fancy that Jane Austen was stronger, sharper, and shrewder than Charlotte Brontë; I am quite sure that she was stronger, sharper, and shrewder than George Eliot. She could do one thing neither of them could do: she could coolly and sensibly describe a man."

—*G. K. Chesterton*

Jane Austen's house in Chawton has become a historical landmark and museum where tourists can visit and view memorabilia of Austen's. The house was first opened as a museum in 1949. For more information about this historic site, visit www.jane-austens-house-museum.org.uk.

Trivia

Jane Austen published *Sense and Sensibility* at her own expense. Published through Thomas Egerton in 1811, Austen was not only able to see her first work in print but also covered the publishing costs and made £140 in profit.

MARRIAGE AND MATTERS OF *the Heart*

"It is not time or opportunity that is to determine intimacy; it is disposition alone. Seven years would be insufficient to make some people acquainted with each other, and seven days are more than enough for others."

—*Marianne Dashwood in* Sense and Sensibility

"Carried her down the hill"

Chapter IX

Sense and Sensibility

MARRIAGE AND MATTERS OF *the Heart*

"Happiness in marriage is entirely a matter of chance. If the dispositions of the parties are ever so well known to each other, or ever so similar before-hand, it does not advance their felicity in the least. They always continue to grow sufficiently unlike afterwards to have their share of vexation; and it is better to know as little as possible of the defects of the person with whom you are to pass your life."

—*Charlotte Lucas in* Pride and Prejudice

Jane Austen's novels appealed to all sorts of people, men and women of all religions. Benjamin Disraeli, the first Jewish prime minister and an author himself, was known to be a fan of Jane Austen's works.

THE FABRIC OF LIFE: *Fashion and Manners*

A lady never called on a gentleman, unless the nature of the call was a business meeting.

THE *Juvenilia*

Jack and Alice (written between 1787 and 1790) is another parody of the novels of the time, this one featuring a heroine with "many rare and charming qualities, but Sobriety is not one of them." The story opens with, "Mr Johnson was once upon a time about 53; in a twelve-month afterwards he was 54, which so much delighted him that he was determined to celebrate his next Birth day by giving a Masquerade to his Children & Friends."

Jane's WORLD

King George III was the reigning monarch throughout Jane's short life. However, King George III's reign was not a run-of-the-mill one. In addition to being blamed for losing the American colonies, he also lost control of his throne. In the early 1800s, George began to show signs of dementia. His son, the future King George IV, took over in 1811 as regent, thus beginning the years called the Regency period in England.

"She writes big truths about little scenes."

—*Elizabeth Bowen on Jane Austen*

Jane's favorite brother, Henry, was her partner in dealing with publishers and was responsible for seeing through the publications of *Northanger Abbey* and *Persuasion* after Jane's death.

"Jane Austen can in fact get more drama out of morality than most other writers can get from shipwreck, battle, murder, or mayhem."

—*Ronald Blythe*

FURTHER READING FOR THOSE WHO CAN'T GET ENOUGH

Mrs. Darcy's Dilemma

by Diana Birchall (2004)

Pride and Prejudice continues twenty-five years later. The well-loved characters are more mature, though not entirely wiser, with children of their own.

AUSTENIAN *Insults*

"Their tempers became their mutual punishment."

—*from* Mansfield Park

UP CLOSE AND *Personal*

The Cambridge Companion to Jane Austen

edited by Edward Copeland and Juliet McMaster (1997)

More than just a biography, this work includes the differing opinions of Austen scholars and essays on the politics, religion, class, and culture of her time.

AT THE *Movies*

Mansfield Park (1999)

Frances O'Connor stars as Fanny Price and, in a more subtle light, Jane Austen herself. While this adaptation does recreate the basic story line, liberties were taken with the material to weave in biographical information about Austen.

Jane's READING

One of Jane's favorite novelists was Fanny Burney. Austen alluded to Burney's characters and novels in her own writings, and she even took the title *Pride and Prejudice* from Burney's *Cecilia*.

AUSTENIAN *Insults*

"Mrs. Hall, of Sherborne, was brought to bed yesterday of a dead child, some weeks before she expected, owing to a fright. I suppose she happened unawares to look at her husband."

—from a letter to her sister

Jane's Life

Sea-bathing was very popular in Jane's time, and she enjoyed visiting several seaside resorts herself. Jane's last novel (unfinished due to her death), SANDITON, features the emergence of a new seaside resort.

Jane's Life

Jane Austen's father, George Austen, was a Church of England clergyman. George supported his daughter's interest in writing and provided her with an education that was broader than what most women received during that time. He even went so far as to offer FIRST IMPRESSIONS, *which would later become* PRIDE AND PREJUDICE, *to a publisher, but the publisher refused to even look at it.*

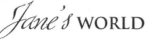Jane's WORLD

Courtship was a very strict endeavor with many rules and prohibitions. In *Sense and Sensibility*, Marianne and Willoughby defy these conventions by riding alone together, using each other's Christian names, and writing to one another.

"I know the summer will pass happily away."

—*Marianne Dashwood in* Sense and Sensibility

AUSTENIAN *Insults*

"What wicked people dyers are. They begin with dipping their own souls in scarlet sin."

—*from a letter to her sister*

Jane's Life

Jane's youngest brother, Charles, followed in Frank's footsteps and joined the navy at a young age, later becoming an admiral, and fought in the Napoleonic Wars.

FURTHER READING FOR THOSE WHO CAN'T GET ENOUGH

An Assembly Such as This
by Pamela Aidan (2003)
A fix for those Darcymania fiends, this novel reveals the first third of *Pride and Prejudice* from Mr. Darcy's point of view.

Trivia

J. K. Rowling, author of the *Harry Potter* series, cites Austen as one of her influences and has read through *Emma* "at least twenty times."

MARRIAGE AND MATTERS OF *the Heart*

"Warmth and tenderness of heart, with an affectionate, open manner, will beat all the cleverness of head in the world, for attraction: I am sure it will."

—*Emma Woodhouse in* Emma

THE FABRIC OF LIFE: *Fashion and Manners*

Undergarments during the Regency period were actually less restrictive than those of earlier and later periods. Due to the shape of the gowns ladies wore, corsets and stays went out of fashion. Instead, ladies wore a modified pantaloon, which was often of a nude or flesh color, making the wearer look as though she weren't wearing any underwear at all.

Trivia

Following the death of Austen's father, Jane, Cassandra, and their mother moved to Clifton, where they lived on an income of approximately £450, which was considered to be barely enough for just one woman of their class, much less three.

Jane's WORLD

Card games were a popular form of entertainment, and characters in Austen's novels are often seen playing them. Some of the most popular card games were whist, loo, and piquet. Gambling often factored into the game and many a lord and lady ran up huge debts resulting in scandal.

AT THE  *Movies*

Pride and Prejudice (2003)

In this modern-day adaptation, Elizabeth Bennet (Kam Heskin) is a studious college student determined not to marry until she graduates. But playboy Wickham (Henry Macguire) and businessman Darcy (Orlando Seale) throw a wrench in the works and thwart her best efforts at keeping her life in order.

" 'Read it aloud,' said their father"
Chap. XLIX

Pride and Prejudice

THE *Juvenilia*

Evelyn (written between 1792 and 1793) is a reflection on excess and greed versus limited resources and restraint. The tale begins with, "In a retired part of the County of Sussex there is a village (for what I know to the Contrary) called Evelyn, perhaps one of the most beautiful Spots in the south of England."

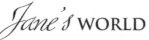 WORLD

At the time of Jane's birth in December of 1775, the British Empire was experiencing serious difficulties with its colonies in the Americas. Fighting had broken out, and in August 1775 the king had declared a state of rebellion; by the end of the year, all colonial trade was banned. The affair was considered a civil conflict, however, not yet a struggle for autonomy. By the time Jane was seven months old, the colonists in America had signed the Declaration of Independence, rejecting imperial rule.

AUSTENIAN *Insults*

"An old married man—quite good for nothing."

—*Mr. Elton in* Emma

FURTHER READING FOR THOSE WHO CAN'T GET ENOUGH

Jane Fairfax

by Joan Aiken (1991)

A retelling of *Emma* through the perspective of Austen's mysterious secondary heroine, Jane Fairfax.

Jane's WORLD

Although the lady and gentleman of the house had relatively little to do, servants and agricultural workers worked nearly all day, from dawn until dusk, for a paltry wage. Jane herself had daily chores around the house, including setting the copper kettle to boil every morning for breakfast.

"You are extremely kind" replied Miss Bates.
Chapter XIX

Emma

"The work of Jane Austen is the Rosetta Stone of literature."

—*Anna Quindlen*

Trivia

The 1995 A&E/BBC production of *Pride and Prejudice* in all its glory had a minor flaw: Jane Bennet opens an envelope containing a note from Caroline Bingley. Envelopes were not yet thought of in Austen's day. Letters were instead written on large sheets of paper, folded into quarters, and sealed with wax. In trying to fit as much as possible on one sheet, some would continue their words at right angles across the previously written words.

AUSTENIAN *Insults*

"You have delighted us long enough."

—*Mr. Bennet in* Pride and Prejudice

UP CLOSE AND *Personal*

Jane Austen in Hollywood

edited by Linda Troost and Sayre Greenfield (second edition, 2001)

The explosion of Austen adaptations begged for the creation of this book. Essays delve into the feminist slants, the manipulations of the novels, and the reason for the sudden interest in Austen.

 WORLD

An accomplished lady or gentleman of the times was expected to know the complicated maneuvers involved in group dances. One had to be careful of one's choice of partner, for partners were usually paired for two consecutive dances, which could last half an hour.

"Let Jane Austen be named the greatest artist that has ever written."

—*George Henry Lewes*

Jane's WORLD

In Jane Austen's time, only the very wealthy could afford their own carriages, thus having a carriage was a sign of prestige. All able-bodied gentlemen were expected to be competent horsemen. Lack of horse or carriage meant that one had to walk. In a famous scene in *Pride and Prejudice*, Elizabeth Bennet walks the three miles to Netherfield, provoking malicious Caroline Bingley to remark, "I hope you saw her petticoat, six inches deep in mud, I am absolutely certain."

AT THE *Movies*

Clueless (1995)

Not just another breezy teen chick flick! This is Jane Austen's *Emma* transplanted to modern Beverly Hills, where Cher (played by Alicia Silverstone), our Emma, loves to play the matchmaker, and has "the power of having rather too much her own way."

THE FABRIC OF LIFE:
Fashion and Manners

A lady would never have worn diamonds or pearls during the morning hours.

FURTHER READING FOR THOSE WHO CAN'T GET ENOUGH

Version and Diversion
by Judith Terry (1986)
Mansfield Park is retold through the perspective of a maid within the household, airing the family's dirty laundry.

AUSTENIAN *Insults*

"A clergyman has nothing to do but be slovenly and self-ish; read the newspaper, watch the weather, and quarrel with his wife. His curate does all the work and the business of his own life is to dine."

—*Miss Crawford in* Mansfield Park

"He.... left them only at the door"
Chap XLI

Mansfield Park

Jane Austen almost always gave her characters the names of real British families that were of high society in her time. For example, Mr. Fitzwilliam Darcy's name was taken from two prominent families of England at the time, the Fitzwilliams and the D'Arcys. Other names that Austen adapted from the aristocracy of Britain include the Bertram family and the Wentsworths.

"Let other pens dwell on guilt and misery."

—*from* Mansfield Park

 ## Jane's WORLD

Medicine was still in its rudimentary stages during Jane Austen's lifetime. However, books touted various home remedies for ailments of the day, including cures for "Distemper got by an ill Husband," "Piles," and "Swelling of the Face."

Trivia

A first edition of *Pride and Prejudice* set an auction record going for £23,500 in 2001. This record was shattered a year later in 2002, when another first edition of *Pride and Prejudice* was sold for £40,000.

Jane's WORLD

Coming out in society was an important event in a girl's life. This meant that she was able to hit the social scene, attend parties, and look for Mr. Right. The girls of the higher classes were presented at court, while others were introduced to society during a ball.

"Miss Austen's novels are perfect works on small scale—beautiful bits of stippling."

—*Alfred, Lord Tennyson*

THE FABRIC OF LIFE:
Fashion and Manners

The period in which Jane Austen lived was governed by strict codes of etiquette. For example, men were not to smoke in the presence of ladies or clergymen, nor on the street in the daylight.

Jane's WORLD

In spite of the tranquil nature of Jane Austen's novels, the world during her lifetime was experiencing great change. The U.S. gained independence and entered the Federalist period. France was heading toward a bloody and violent revolution and spawning its greatest military leader whose grandiose ambitions would be felt across Europe. England itself was experiencing the pains of progress with the advent of the Industrial Revolution. Perhaps the quiet, everydayness of Jane's characters' lives made her novels a happy respite for an anxious and turbulent world.

"The General attended her himself to the street door"
Chap XIII

Northanger Abbey

AUSTENIAN *Insults*

"I do not write for such dull elves, as they have not a great deal of ingenuity themselves."

—from a letter to Martha Lloyd

"I haven't any right to criticize books, and I don't do it except when I hate them. I often want to criticize Jane Austen, but her books madden me so that I can't conceal my frenzy from the reader; and therefore I have to stop every time I begin. Every time I read *Pride and Prejudice* I want to dig her up and beat her over the skull with her own shin-bone."

—Mark Twain

AT THE *Movies*

Persuasion (1995)

Amanda Root stars as the quietly patient Anne Elliot. Though the movie may seem to move rather slowly, the subtle performances and body language—especially the looks!—keep you captivated when dialogue isn't present.

AUSTENIAN *Insults*

"I was as civil to them as their bad breath would allow me."

—*from a letter to her sister*

"If charity is the poetry of conduct and honor the rhetoric of conduct, then Jane Austen's 'principles' might be described as the grammar of conduct."

—*C. S. Lewis*

AT THE MOVIES

Pride and Prejudice (1980)

In this adaptation, David Rintoul's Mr. Darcy is stiff and gruff, although certainly handsome, and his portrayal contrasts the witty, charming, and lively Elizabeth (played by Elizabeth Garvie) perfectly.

Jane's Life

Jane's brother George was mentally retarded and prone to fits, and was sent to live with laboring people in a nearby village. Being excluded from family life, he and Jane were not very close.

FURTHER READING FOR THOSE WHO CAN'T GET ENOUGH

Excessively Diverted

by Juliette Shapiro (2002)

The happily-ever-after ending for the Darcys doesn't ring true in this continuation of *Pride and Prejudice* as they brace themselves against one dramatic event after another.

THE FABRIC OF LIFE:
Fashion and Manners

An unmarried woman under the age of thirty was never to exchange correspondence with a man before she was engaged to him.

FURTHER READING FOR THOSE WHO CAN'T GET ENOUGH

Old Friends and New Fancies
by Sybil G. Brinton (1913)
The first sequel to any of Austen's novels. The story focuses on Colonel Fitzwilliam, Kitty Bennet, and Georgiana Darcy of *Pride and Prejudice* but weaves in all the best-loved characters of Austen's novels.

"Beware of swoons…Run mad as often as you chuse; but do not faint."

—*Sophia in* Love and Freindship *[sic]*

"Oh God! her father and mother!"
Chapter XII

Persuasion

AT THE *Movies*

Colin Firth inspired Darcymania with his portrayal of the complicated and charmingly enigmatic Mr. Darcy in the 1995 A&E/BBC miniseries of *Pride and Prejudice*. Firth had never read *Pride and Prejudice* and almost turned down the role, until he was told that Darcy was one of the sexiest characters in English literature.

UP CLOSE AND *Personal*

Jane Austen: A Family Record
by William Austen-Leigh, Richard Austen-Leigh, and Deirdre Le Faye (1989)
This is an updated and expanded version of the 1913 original by the Austen-Leighs, detailing Austen's role within her family and how the events of her life were woven into her novels.

Jane's Life

Jane was almost sent to prison! There are rumors that Austen's mother offered Jane and Cassandra as companions to their aunt Jane Leigh-Perrot while she was in prison, having been accused of stealing a card of lace.

UP CLOSE AND *Personal*

Becoming Jane Austen

by Jon Spence (2003)

Broadening the scope of Jane's life, this work takes a look at the lives and events of those around her and how they are woven into her novels.

"I am a Jane Austenite, and therefore slightly imbecile about Jane Austen. My fatuous expression, and airs of personal immunity—how ill they sit on the face, say, of a Stevensonian! But Jane Austen is so different. She is my favourite author! I read and reread, the mouth open and the mind closed. Shut up in measureless content, I greet her by the name of most kind hostess, while criticism slumbers."

—*E. M. Forster*

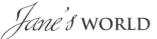 WORLD

Men's lives during the Regency period were quite active. They participated in outdoor pursuits such as hunting, fishing, and riding. Their days were spent managing their estates. Women of the upper classes, however, had to battle boredom daily. Not permitted to do any work around the house or on the estate, they would paint, read, or engage in the feminine art of embroidery.

FURTHER READING FOR THOSE WHO CAN'T GET ENOUGH

Jane Austen Mysteries

by Stephanie Barron

This series of seven books weaves in excerpts from Austen's life as Jane Austen the sleuth uses her gifts of perception to unravel mysteries. For instance, in *Jane and the Prisoner of Wool House*, Jane must prove the innocence of a family friend before he hangs for a murder he did not commit.

AT THE *Movies*

Emma (1996)

Gwyneth Paltrow's accent may be a bit jarring in this adaptation of *Emma*, but all is forgiven for her superb portrayal of the mischievous and misguided heroine who insists on playing matchmaker to all those around her—and Jeremy Northam's handsome and charming Mr. Knightley cannot be missed!

Jane's WORLD

If a woman wished to marry, she needed to heighten her attractiveness by being accomplished in as many arts as possible. Jane took piano lessons, and Cassandra learned to draw. Of course, both girls were schooled in the art of dancing as well. According to Miss Caroline Bingley in *Pride and Prejudice*, an accomplished woman "must have a thorough knowledge of music, singing, drawing, dancing, and the modern languages, to deserve the word; and besides all this, she must possess a certain something in her air and manner of walking, the tone of her voice, her address and expressions, or the word will be but half deserved." When Mr. Darcy added, "…she must yet add something more substantial, in the improvement of her mind by extensive reading," Lizzie Bennet retorted, "I am no longer surprised at your knowing *only* six accomplished women. I rather wonder now at your knowing *any*."

Jane's Life

Jane's brother Edward was adopted by rich relatives and later changed his surname to Knight. Because of his wealthy inheritance, he was able to help his mother and sisters financially after Reverend Austen died.

FURTHER READING FOR THOSE WHO CAN'T GET ENOUGH

Presumption
by Julia Barrett (1993)
This sequel to *Pride and Prejudice* focuses on the romantic interludes of Georgiana, Mr. Darcy's younger sister, as she tries to choose between two suitors.

" _With a letter in her outstretched hand_ "

Chapter XXXI

Sense and Sensibility

Jane's Life

The Austen family frequently held theatricals in their home, and Mrs. Austen insisted that all members of the family present should act. The Austen family was known to be excellent at writing and performing charades, and they practiced often as a pastime. Many of Jane's earlier works were written for the evening pleasure of her family.

UP CLOSE AND *Personal*

Jane Austen: Her Life

by Park Honan (1988)

This biography asserts that Jane was far from the sheltered young woman many believed her to be. Instead, she was quite aware of the exciting (and dangerous!) events going on around her—events that found their way into her works.

In the 1995 film version of *Sense and Sensibility*, Edward Ferrars makes a reference to Vladivostok, a city founded in 1860. However, the actual story of *Sense and Sensibility* was set in 1810.

THE FABRIC OF LIFE: *Fashion and Manners*

A gentleman always ascended stairs in front of a lady and descended the stairs following her.

FURTHER READING FOR THOSE WHO CAN'T GET ENOUGH

A Goodly Heritage: A History of Jane Austen's Family and
Jane Austen the Woman

by George Tucker (1983 and 1994)

"She was a full-blooded woman, not just a shadow." George Tucker is recognized by the Jane Austen Society of North America as being one of the top authorities on Jane Austen. His biographies are rich with little-known facts about Austen and her family, and paint Austen in a colorful light, claiming she was a lively woman who was very much aware of current events.

Jane's WORLD

Family breakfasts? Not in Regency England. Men rose earlier and ate in the dining room. Women either ate in their rooms by themselves or later in the morning with other women.

THE FABRIC OF LIFE:
Fashion and Manners

Jane was an admirer of the fashionable when it was available to her. She had two particularly favorite bonnets that she longed to wear to important balls. The first was a black velvet ruffled cap that she would borrow from Cassandra when she was away from home. The other was a bonnet with a narrow silver ribbon wrapped twice around the crown, without a bow to tie it, and a feather that stood up at the side. Jane Austen was a fan of the color *coquelicot*, which was a bright pink.

FURTHER READING FOR THOSE WHO CAN'T GET ENOUGH

A Visit to Highbury
by Joan Austen-Leigh (1995)
The great-granddaughter of Austen's nephew retells the story of Emma from the point of view of Mary Goddard, mistress of a boarding school, through an exchange of letters with her younger sister.

Trivia

Jane Austen was not known as a wonderful speller. She always confused the placement of *i* and *e* within words. She particularly had problems with the words believe, receive, piece, and niece, which her editors had continually to change, and which are noticeable in the remaining letters to her sister.

Jane's Life

When Jane was just thirty-seven years old, she wrote to her sister, "I bought a concert ticket and a sprig of flowers for my old age."

AT THE *Movies*

Emma (1997)

This A&E miniseries stars Kate Beckinsale as the match-making Emma and Samantha Morton as the shy Harriet Smith. Having been released less than a year following the glamorous Hollywood production of *Emma*, it took some hits from critics for its more reserved characterizations, but most agree that this version is truer to Austen's novel.

MARRIAGE AND MATTERS OF *the Heart*

"Lady Sondes's match surprises, but does not offend me; had her first marriage been of affection, or had there been a grown-up single daughter, I should not have forgiven her; but I consider everybody as having a right to marry once in their lives for love, if they can, and provided she will now leave off having bad headaches and being pathetic, I can allow her, I can wish her, to be happy."

—*from a letter to her sister*

"Standing together over the hearth."
Chap. LV.

Pride and Prejudice

UP CLOSE AND *Personal*

The Friendly Jane Austen
by Natalie Tyler (1999)
A light and user-friendly introduction to Austen, complete with quizzes, bio, interviews with actors and scholars, and entertaining illustrations.

"Nothing amuses me more than the easy manner with which everybody settles the abundance of those who have a great deal less than themselves."

—*Miss Crawford in* Mansfield Park

Jane's WORLD

Britain was at war with France during most of Jane's adult life. Having two brothers in the Royal Navy led Jane to take a great interest in the battles taking place. She took many opportunities in *Persuasion* to honor those who fought for their country.

THE FABRIC OF LIFE:
Fashion and Manners

"Certainly she had often, especially of late, thought his manners to herself unnecessarily gallant; but it had passed as his way, as a mere error of judgment, of knowledge, of taste, as one proof among others that he had not always lived in the best society, that with all the gentleness of his address, true elegance was sometimes wanting."

—*from* Emma

Jane's love for the sea began when she received letters from her brother, Charles, who was a sailor. It was his letters that prompted her to spend time away from home on the seashore when she was young. Charles gave her a favorite piece of jewelry—a topaz cross on a gold chain. When she held it, she dreamed that she held the ocean.

FURTHER READING FOR THOSE WHO CAN'T GET ENOUGH

Mr. Darcy's Daughters

by Elizabeth Aston (2003)

Pride and Prejudice continues twenty-one years later with the five marriageable daughters of the Darcys who must contend with the temptations and romances of Regency London, while their parents travel to Constantinople (of all places!).

Jane Austen's novels focus almost exclusively on the rural gentry. Some of the gentry were titled, but most were not. Those titles available to the gentry were baronet, knight, and lady. While Jane focused on the minor gentry in her works, she also included titled characters such as Sir Thomas Bertram and Lady Catherine de Bourgh.

Jane's Life

Jane's character was influenced early on by her practical and amusing mother, who wore a scarlet riding habit as her wedding outfit. She was speculated to be a great rider in her time, but would not be able to ride a horse for years to come because she and her husband planned on having a big family, and pregnancy was not conducive to horseback riding.

AUSTENIAN *Insults*

"She is a cold-hearted, vain woman."

—*Edmund Bertram in* Mansfield Park

UP CLOSE AND *Personal*

Jane Austen: A Biography

by Elizabeth Jenkins (1938)

As the first detailed biography written by someone outside of the Austen family, this book is valuable to Austen enthusiasts who want to read an objective view of her life, era, class, and inspirations.

AT THE *Movies*

Persuasion (1971)

This adaptation takes its time to faithfully recreate Austen's novel. The scenes are subtle and the actors do not perform with a dramatic flair, but this simply works to bring Austen's words to the forefront.

Trivia

Jane Austen's works have been translated into at least thirty-five languages and have never been out of print.

Jane's WORLD

Women in Austen's day had very few options. Most women deemed it necessary to attempt to marry as well as possible, even if this meant marrying a man she could barely tolerate. Austen's opinion on this subject can be seen in her characterization of Charlotte Lucas's attitude to marriage with the revolting Mr. Collins in *Pride and Prejudice*: "Mr. Collins to be sure was neither sensible nor agreeable; his society was irksome, and his attachment to her must be imaginary. But still he would be her husband. Without thinking highly either of men or matrimony, marriage had always been her object; it was the only honourable provision for well-educated young women of small fortune, and however uncertain of giving happiness, must be their pleasantest preservation."

Jane's Life

Jane's favorite poet was William Cowper. Though their personalities were quite the opposite—the former cheerful and the latter melancholy—they shared a love for simple pleasures. Austen gave Cowper to both Fanny Price and Marianne Dashwood in her novels.

FURTHER READING FOR THOSE WHO CAN'T GET ENOUGH

Mansfield Revisited

by Joan Aiken (1984)

This sequel to *Mansfield Park* takes Fanny and Edmund to Antigua, leaving Susan Price behind to deal with the daily dramas at Mansfield Park.

Jane's Life

Jane Austen never married; however, she did receive a proposal of marriage on December 2, 1802, from Harris Bigg-Wither, a wealthy landowner and a friend of the family. Austen accepted the younger man's proposal (Bigg-Wither was a mere twenty-one to Austen's twenty-seven years). Following a sleepless night, Austen decided that she simply could not marry without love and withdrew her acceptance the very next morning.

Jane's NAME

In December of 1817, "Jane Austen" appeared in print for the first time in the preface, written by her brother Henry, of *Persuasion* and *Northanger Abbey*, which were printed together in four volumes.

"I think I may boast myself to be, with all possible vanity, the most unlearned and uninformed female who ever dared to be an authoress."

—*from a letter to James Clarke dated December 11, 1815*

The Jane Austen Centre in Bath, England, pays homage to one of its most famous residents. Visitors can go on a walking tour of the town where Jane's characters strolled as well as have their photographs taken in Regency attire. For more information, visit www.janeausten.co.uk.

"The enjoyment of Elinor's company"
Chapter XLIX

Sense and Sensibility

THE FABRIC OF LIFE:
Fashion and Manners

A lady never accepted a gift from a man to whom she was not engaged.

UP CLOSE AND *Personal*

Jane Austen's World
by Maggie Lane (1996)
This biography of Austen describes not only the important events and people in Jane's life, but also the social conventions, wars, and fashions of her lifetime.

"In Miss A[usten]'s works, & especially in *M[ansfield] P[ark]*, you actually live with them, you fancy yourself one of the family; & the scenes are so exactly descriptive, so perfectly natural, that there is scarcely an Incident, or conversation, or a person, that you are not inclined to imagine you have at one time or other in your Life been a witness to, borne a part in, & been acquainted with."

—Lady Gordon

Jane's WORLD

Bath was a hot spot for the fashionable, known for its healing waters. Jane, however, wasn't at all happy at her father's decision to retire to Bath in December of 1800 and is said to have fainted at the mention of it. Austen's feelings about this move can be seen in *Persuasion*'s Anne Elliot.

AT THE *Movies*

Emma (1972)

This BBC miniseries production of Austen's *Emma* takes its time in developing the characters and plot, and follows the novel quite closely. Such great care with Austen's well-crafted dialogue and characters can only be applauded.

FURTHER READING FOR THOSE WHO CAN'T GET ENOUGH

Consequence

by Elizabeth Newark (1997)

Charlotte Lucas's story continues in this sequel to *Pride and Prejudice*. The Darcys and Collinses are brought together once again when their offspring share a romance.

"I do not want people to be very agreeable, as it saves me the trouble of liking them a great deal."

—*from a letter to her sister*

Jane Austen died in her sister's arms at the too-young age of forty-one and was buried in Winchester Cathedral. Her inscription reads: "In memory of JANE AUSTEN, youngest daughter of the late Revd. GEORGE AUSTEN, formerly Rector of Steventon in this County. She departed this Life on the 18th of July 1817, aged 41, after a long illness supported with the patience and the hopes of a Christian. The benevolence of her heart, the sweetness of her temper, and the extraordinary endowments of her mind obtained the regard of all who knew her, and the warmest love of her intimate connections. Their grief is in proportion to their affection, they know their loss to be irreparable, but in the deepest affliction they are consoled by a firm though humble hope that her charity, devotion, faith, and purity have rendered her soul acceptable in the sight of her REDEEMER."

Since the original inscription on Austen's tomb mentions nothing of her work as a writer, another brass tablet was added to her grave later, which reads: "Jane Austen. Known to many by her writings, endeared to her family by the varied charms of her character and ennobled by her Christian faith and piety was born at Steventon in the County of Hants, December 16 1775 and buried in the Cathedral July 18 1817. 'She openeth her mouth with wisdom and in her tongue is the law of kindness.'"

"Jane lies in Winchester—blessed be her shade! Praise the Lord for making her, and her for all she made! And while the stones of Winchester, or Milsom Street, remain, Glory, love, and honour unto England's Jane!"

—epitaph written to "The Janeites"
by Rudyard Kipling